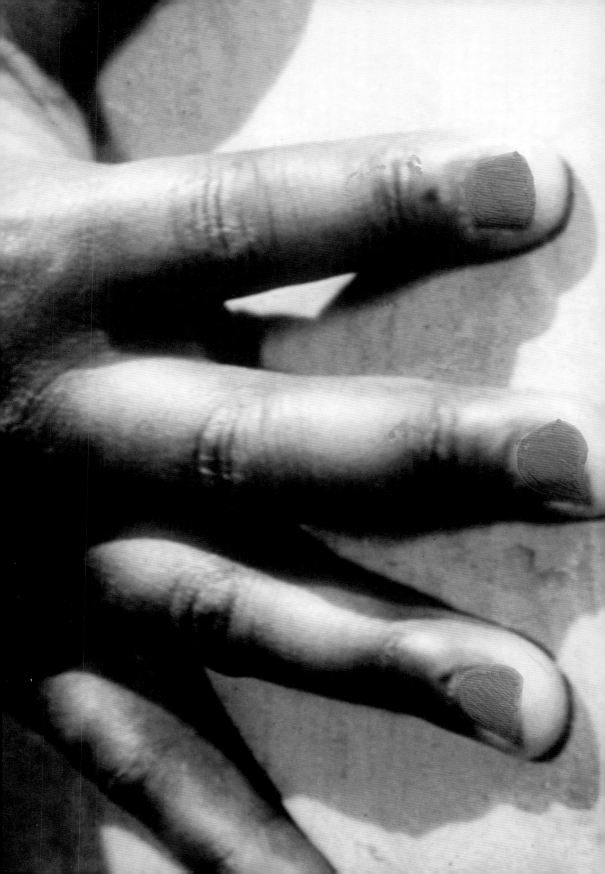

STEVE McQUEEN

ICA
INSTITUTE OF CONTEMPORARY ARTS
LONDON

KUNSTHALLE
ZÜRICH

ISBN 1 900300 17 6

UK and Europe:
ICA Exhibitions
12 Carlton House Terrace
London SW1Y 5AH
Distributed by
Cornerhouse Publications
70 Oxford Street
Manchester M1 5NH
USA and worldwide excluding UK and Europe:
Distributed by **D.A.P.**
(Distributed Art Publishers)
636 Broadway, 1st Floor
New York NY 10012

Published by the ICA in collaboration with the Kunsthalle Zürich to coincide with the exhibition STEVE McQUEEN,
30 January - 21 March, 1999, Institute of Contemporary Arts, London
12 June - 15 August, 1999, Kunsthalle Zürich

©ICA, Kunsthalle Zürich, STEVE McQUEEN, ROBERT STORR, MICHAEL NEWMAN, OKWUI ENWEZOR, 1999
All works © The Artist, Anthony Reynolds Gallery, London and Marian Goodman Gallery, Paris/New York.

Edited by GERRIE VAN NOORD
Designed by LUC DERYCKE
Printed by ARTEPRINT, Brussels

cover image:
Deadpan, 1997
All images courtesy the Artist, Anthony Reynolds Gallery, London and Marian Goodman Gallery, Paris/New York

CONTENTS

GOING PLACES

Robert Storr

*M*oving pictures. That's what they are, and that is what they do. At any rate, that is what Steve McQueen's pictures are and do.

In English-speaking countries we inherit this expression from the early days of the medium. At that time, only the French called it 'cinema'. The French have a way with words and their way simultaneously tends to make things sound more important and less physical, less 'thingy'. Which is why the French win arguments, but, with obvious exceptions, create so few moving pictures that can compete with the more matter-of-fact products of their neighbours in Germany, Italy, and Great Britain, not to mention the restless Americans they alternately idolise and condescend to. But enough of that. The reason that the term 'moving pictures' suits its purpose so well is the historical point it implicitly makes. Previously requiring no qualifier, pictures used to be static. What motion they contained was a matter of artful illusion. The airborne horses that flew across the ground in equestrian paintings of the eighteenth and nineteenth century were pure fiction, as Eadweard Muybridge took pains to demonstrate in his sequential, proto-filmic photographs of galloping steeds.

Nowadays, with TV, digitised billboards, and 'media' in general, it is remarkable when pictures don't move. This leaves canvas-bound artists to play ruefully with the ironies of their new situation. I am thinking, for example, of David Hockney's depiction of a tiger leaping at an apparently unsuspecting man. Asked by a worried spectator about this calamity-in-the-making Hockney explained that there was no cause for alarm since the ambush took place in a painting where, by definition, the tiger would remain eternally suspended above its prey unable to lay tooth or claw upon him.

Linking Steve McQueen to David Hockney may strike the reader, especially the British reader, as too much of a stretch or, worse, the tell-tale sign of American provincialism according to which 'London' is an aesthetic criterion. However, the truth of the matter is that my primary imaginative realm is that of *un*moving pictures and, as a consequence, I am alert not only to signs of motion in those that hang on a wall, but of stillness or inertial tempos in those which flicker on a screen, or in McQueen's case, on gallery and museum walls normally occupied by fixed images. In such instances one feels the tug of history, and of the conventions of interrupted dramatic gesture and accentuated spatial dynamics that suggest the unfolding of actions which movies straightforwardly show.

There is a good deal of this tension in McQueen's early work. Even the casual rep cinema-goer or video-renter will recognise in these enigmatic black and white narratives the impact of Sergei Eisenstein, Orson Welles, and the formally strict but visually grand tradition of film-making they personify. Extreme, even caricatural foreshortening, sharp but optically luxurious *chiaroscuro* prolonged attention to a head or body that holds itself steady for the camera until, suddenly, it or the camera lurches, breaking the current that inscribes the image with laser intensity in the mind's eye of the viewer. Then there are tableau-like compositions in which such film-makers specialised, compositions which never lost their choreographic balance or clarity of articulation, no matter how violent the events they described.

Behind Eisenstein and Welles, as well as behind *film noir*, the streetwise modernist extension of the 'high' modernist style they invented, lies Baroque painting. The angle 'shots' of Veronese, the variously shadowy or revelatory 'lighting' of Caravaggio, the charged, set-piece deployment of figures in both, and then, at an aesthetic tangent to these Italian masters, the distancing regard of Velázquez, and his attentiveness to what happens when uninflected emptiness surrounds a hard material reality. Baroque painting is the art of the exceptional rendered as the ordinary, of the extreme experiences and eccentric views of the world bodied forth as if they had merely been seen rather than elaborately contrived. A fusion of naturalism and exaggeration, the Baroque was ready-made for appropriation by film which was ready-made for both.

Movies therefore owe painting a lot, but painting will never collect in full. Instead, recognition of the debt comes in the form of self-consciously pictorial films of the type already referred to, 'classics' that even in their day often seemed as backward-looking in their frame by frame vision as they were advanced in their technical transposition of painterly effects sprocketed onto celluloid. Latter-day recourse to such devices by a young artist thus contains an element of redoubled anachronism or displacement, especially at a moment when the supposed authenticity of 'Minicam-vérité' informs so much of current film and video output. Choosing to make *his* moving pictures in an explicitly dramatic idiom that insistently evokes both film history and art history, McQueen has taken a gamble few of his contemporaries have been prepared to consider. That he has managed to make some of the most arresting 'shorts' in recent memory is proof not only that McQueen fully comprehends the precedents involved – which, for a working artist as opposed to a critic or scholar, means having a keen sense for what is still useful and what has been, for the time being at least, used up – but he has done so without obvious 'pomo' irony, the attitudinal uniform of this generation's academics. Rather, McQueen's work is distinguished by an emotionally charged directness that claims his elective affinities with the past for our common present.

His first important film, *Bear* (1993), is an ambiguously physical encounter between two naked men, who trade looks at each other by way of the camera, egg one another on, cuff each other, gently embrace, lock arms and heads in inconclusive struggle, and then circle in an athletic *pas de deux* version of a pugilistic standoff. A ritual street corner squaring off performed in the nude as if the antagonists were animated marble wrestlers from some Roman statue, the sequence is a study in male restraint with cross-cutting undercurrents of latent violence and affection.

Similar in style, *Five Easy Pieces* (1995), his second production, has little resemblance to the Bob Rafelson movie after which it was named. Indeed, McQueen had not actually seen the original when he borrowed its title.

The words alone struck him as appropriate to his own brief film 'exercises', which consist of three intercut segments, shot from unusually high or low angles. An upward view of slippered feet walking a tightrope and of a muscular woman in a sequinned and fringed dress concentrating on maintaining her equilibrium; an overhead view of a group of men and women twirling Hula-Hoops; and then an upward view of a man, arms behind his head, languorously swaying his hips to keep his hoop in place that transmutes into a similarly posed image of a man standing in boxer shorts who, in the final sequence, urinates downwards into a basin of water in whose reflection he seems to be standing over the viewer like a colossus.

The exact significance of the scenes in these two films and the reason for their juxtaposition in the latter one remains a mystery, but their visual coherence is immediately apparent. At once intensely sculptural and emphatically cinematic, we find form, lose its contour and therefore its identity, and then rediscover it in faces, torsos, and limbs through the combined action of a roving camera that rotates around the body, and a stationary or almost stationary one that tracks the bodies' movement toward and away from the lens or in and out of its rectangular scope. In the sparring match between the two men, the camera effectively plays the part of a third body, sizing up the combatants, bracketing their dance of assault and evasion, bearing the brunt of a frontal charge by one, and witnessing the sly, fraternal, half-shy, half-easy intimacy between the two apparent adversaries.

The massive woman aerialist, photographed in rich black and white that details the grain of the rope, the creases in her slippers, and the weave of the fabric hugging her bust and hips, and the sparkling fixation in her eyes gives us a similarly eroticised sense of strength harnessed by grace, of equilibrium achieved and maintained by force of will, to which the hula-hoopers play an almost abstract chorus line, suggesting Potemkin remade by Busby Berkeley. And then there is the gigantic, implacable man who takes his morning piss on our heads, scrambling the illusion of unmediated vision as his stream hits the surface of the pool that mirrors him, exploding his likeness. Even this most mundane of acts is lent an aura of monumentality, dignifying the performer of the indignity performed.

Throughout, McQueen regulates the camera speed to underscore energetic *agon* that prepares or plays itself out in each recorded gesture or expression just as the close-cropping of the images and the starkness or vacancy of their backgrounds focuses exclusive attention on the telling detail of movement upon which each section of film hangs. Traditional drama organises such tensions toward a crisis and then resolution. In McQueen's first film, there is no such denouement, no build-up and release. A moving picture without a story, we have lights, camera, action – and ellipsis.

In contrast to *Bear* and *Five Easy Pieces*, *Just Above My Head* (1996) – this time McQueen's title quotes James Baldwin instead of Hollywood – opens the frame wide and pulls back to the point where the image just barely holds a position inside it. The minimalism of McQueen's conception is matched by the stubborn monumentality of his presence and the odd sublimity of his optic. The seven-and-a-half minute film consists of a single tracking shot of the artist walking under an overcast sky, bypassing the occasional tree. When the camera, which looks up to McQueen's head from the level of the road, slightly exceeds his pace, he momentarily drops out of the picture, only to recover his marginal place in our field of vision with the next big stride, which at the other extreme brings at most his shoulders into view. The strangeness of this pictorial 'chinning' is accentuated by the vantage point of the spectator who stands in the darkened cubicle where the film is projected at mural scale, such that one 'looks down to look up' as one watched the

Exodus, 1992 / 1997

bobbing head appear and disappear along the line where the wall meets the floor.

For all the seeming whimsicality of McQueen's pretext, however, *Just Above My Head* has a surprising poignancy. Against the opaque fathomlessness of the clouds, the solitary figure struggling to hold his own is informed by a spiritual as well as literal gravity, a kind of incidental existentialist pathos, which, allied to the impassive determination one sees in the set of the artist's eyes and jaw, makes this a picture parable about not falling behind but always staying on the move. That the title of Baldwin's hymn-cadenced last novel was derived from the lyrics of an old song that goes "Just above my head/I hear music in the air" may or may not have been known to McQueen, but there is a subtly exalted aspect to this otherwise stripped down narrative that would suggest the absence of a soundtrack may have been to the overall metaphor, and silence the most economical and evocative of counter-symbols.

Something old, Something new, Something borrowed, Something blue, (1998) reprises this effortful flight forward in the painfully slow and frankly melodramatic image of a hand reaching out to drag the weight of a body we do not see, as it crawls across a hard, masonry floor, which due to subtle jump-cutting seems to outpace the advancing hand like a receding conveyor-belt. Except for broken shadows and fractured rays of light that fall across this one hand, neither do we see the other. But metonymy completes this image of Sisyphean labour. Beyond its direct but still mysterious application to this short film-sequence – the rhyme belongs to wedding lore – the title phrase summarises the aesthetic coordinates of McQueen's initial projects, which consisted of something old, something new, something borrowed, and, with an always understated but always present accent, something 'blue'.

The fact that McQueen does not make an obvious issue of his race – or that of his predominantly white art world public – is a mark of confident take-it-or-leave-it self-acceptance and of an explicitly political sophistication, which assumes that assertion rather than protest, intelligently structured poetics rather than structuralist 'critique' may be, at this moment, the best means for imparting new or difference-defining information. But McQueen's discretion in this regard complements his manifest attention to the matter of who is pictured and how.

The men engaged in mock battle are black and McQueen surely knows that the sight of black men fighting strikes different nerves differently, just as he knows that their nakedness will not be seen the same way by

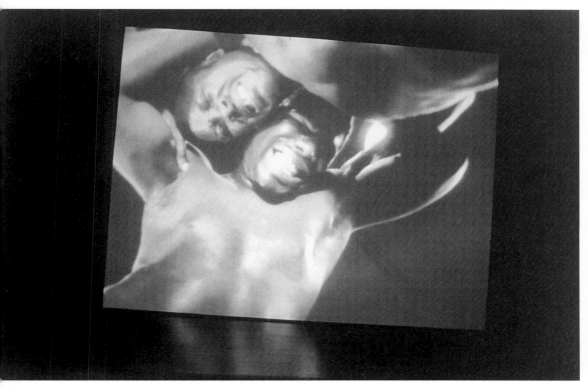

Bear, 1993

the general audience in Britain or America. Similarly, McQueen's tightrope-walker is the antithesis of the traditional circus sylph, but the change in paradigm she represents dictates no single reading of her statuesque presence. And what is one to make of *Exodus* in which two black men carry coconut trees down a London market street on their way to boarding a bus. Unlike his other works, this one records a real event filmed on the fly, but the resonance of the piece makes it more than the cinematic equivalent of 'decisive moment' photography. With its hint of nostalgia or even homesickness – "a palm tree grows in Brick Lane" – and the balletic absurdity of the leaves swaying above the crowd, the vignette resembles a short play by Samuel Beckett with post-colonial overtones.

McQueen, nevertheless, refrains from editorialising. The polyvalence of these images is at the heart of his challenge to the public; and I mean the heart in the sense that a primary emotional reaction is the predicate for critical response rather than an individual psychological sidebar to textual or subtextual analysis. Throughout, the essential emotion McQueen and his surrogates express is self-possession. Nowhere is it more in evidence – and more in question – than in *Deadpan* (1997), whose single, repeated image is based on a slapstick sequence from Buster Keaton's *One Week* (1921) in which the side of a newly constructed house collapses on that most imperturbable of calamity-prone comics, but he is spared because an open window in the façade matches the patch of earth on which he stands. McQueen's re-enactment of the Keaton joke turns dumb luck into a test of courage but above all, of premeditation and will. In *Deadpan*'s four minutes we watch the wall come down several times and return to its upright position once. At first we watch the whole sequence, then only McQueen's feet are visible, then the window, then the drop, followed by several repeats of the action from different angles, then a long close-up of McQueen's unchanging and inscrutable face against a backdrop of flashing black and white shadows as the façade is drawn back into place, and the one last oblique view of the whole cycle that ends in a sudden blackout as the wall seems to land on the camera. Over and over it happens, and throughout, the artist remains immobile, the unflinching focus of a potentially disastrous movement.

In all, it is as if he were being targeted rather than accidentally jeopardised and miraculously saved as was his archetypal counterpart. Indeed he has been – by himself. And, by exposing the mechanics of this sight-gag, and repeating it so that the slim margin for error and full impact of the wall hitting the ground is brought home to the viewer,

McQueen simultaneously underscores the genuine risk inherent in the trick, and his own absolute command of the situation. Though he never registers fear, at each pass of the wall around his rigid form, we can sense both the danger of this self-imposed gamble and the authority exercised to ensure that disaster will not occur. In short, *Deadpan* is a narrative of survival, but more than that, of survival by design. *Just Above My Head* conjures with transcendental longing; *Deadpan* plays on the more plausible fear that at any instant the world may come crashing down around your ears. The first links determination to unlimited horizons, but anchors whatever hope or sense of freedom may be born of this connection to the unceasing difficulty of staying in stride and staying in the picture. The second tempts fate in order to master it.

It is the mark of McQueen's mastery of his medium that he stages such incidents so plainly and summons complex thoughts and emotions so efficiently that the 'literature' of his work does not seem like literature at all, but simply a statement of something that happened, incompletely perhaps, but happened with such vividness that we are drawn in and made to wonder "why". Yet the artist refrains from providing any answers, preferring instead a lapidary language of short takes and pictorial densities that substitute visual immediacy and seeming inevitability for conventional causality.

Drumroll (1998), McQueen's most recent film, represents a significant redirection of the artist's work, away from theatricality toward a more strictly camera-centred spatial dynamics. *Catch* (1997), McQueen's *Documenta* entry of that year signalled this shift. Inspired in part by Dan Graham's *Body Press* (1970-72) in which a couple pass a camera around the surface of their nude bodies, in effect modelling for each other as the apparatus models their contours, *Catch* is a game of toss in which the camera is the ball. On one side of the pitch stands a woman, at the other McQueen himself. Between them the image gyrates in flight, creating kaleidoscopic abstractions, only to be grasped securely and levelled on the torso and face of the catcher's opposite number, who stares into it like someone having their passport picture taken. In *Drumroll*, the human agency of the filming process all but vanishes. What one sees on screen is a triptych, at the centre of which is a masked, round image, and to the left and right are rectangular images. All three are synchronised real-time tapes of what an oil drum 'saw' as it was rolled through the streets of midtown Manhattan. The central image, which whirls with vertiginous speed between sky and pavement – with barely legible flashes of McQueen's head, shirt and pink coat on every full turn – represents the view of a camera in the centre of the barrel, the left and right, which tumble like front-loading washing machines, represent the view of camera set just inside the end rims of the drum and trained outwards at shank level.

Unlike previous films, *Drumroll* has sound, and what one hears is likewise a real-time application of the information provided by the three separate optics; the rumble of the oil drum, the cacophony of traffic, the occasional queries or exclamations of passers-by – "What's happening?!" – and the polite but unyielding voice of McQueen, saying "Excuse me, please", as he literally barrels along.

The immediate fascination of the film is purely visual. A contemporary 'man with a movie camera', McQueen offers an initially disorienting, but in the end formally cohesive and vividly Simultaneist vision of the modern city. But then again one asks, "Which man in which city, on what terms?" Comparison with David Hammons's *Phat Free* (1995-97) is instructive.

In that hauntingly atmospheric tape we see and hear the artist kick a bucket soccer-ball style around the Harlem streets at night. The clatter of the empty container, the aimlessness of the course Hammons follows, the eerie sulphur lamplight on darkened brick and cement, the graininess of the video stock and the feeling of metropolitan anomie all speak of urban nomadism, of marginal geographies and migrations, and indirectly but unmistakably, of the bittersweet 'liberties' of African-American life. McQueen, by contrast, chose to cut a swath straight through Midtown. Fleetingly one glimpses his reflection in the windows and mirrored glass façades of the buildings he trundles past, and it is the reflection of a hulking black man in scarlet, utterly intent on his easily misunderstood purpose of pushing an industrial container through some of the fanciest commercial real estate in New York.

I do not think it is my Americanness alone, and with that my long experience of ethnic and social stereotyping, that makes me sensitive to these apparently incidental indicators. Rather, it strikes me as undeniable that while McQueen is determined to show us something for its own sake, he is as always mindful that who does the showing is a part of the content that is finally absorbed by the viewer. 'No', in theory, an experimental artist's colour should not matter, but 'Yes', when the experiment is run in public space, it does. And so McQueen takes note of himself, and of his voice, and of the patterns of response as he makes his way. A drum roll heralds a ritual or event. In this case, the ritual is making a moving picture that documents a city's exhilarating kinesthesia; the event is a young black movie-maker 'taking' Manhattan without warning, simply because it is there to be taken.

Five Easy Pieces, 1995

18   Typical of all McQueen's various endeavours, which now include
sculpture as well as photography, lies an eloquent capacity for
condensation. Objectifying motion under the pressure of the medium's
optical frame and with a full appreciation of the mass and momentum
of bodies in action, McQueen treats both the subjects he films and the
projected, cinematic result as physical realities in that they occupy
space in an absolute way, even as they move within it. Modern painters
– regardless of whether their work is abstract or figurative –
understand that they must pay close attention to the manner in which
the materials they employ impose themselves upon the viewer and
upon the other material facts in their environs. Run-of-the-mill films
have in effect fallen for all the illusions that painting has learned to
forswear. Not so the moving pictures of Steve McQueen. Classically
'modern' in that they put the medium on display, they nevertheless
exploit inherited pictorial options that recent avant-gardes have left
unexamined. And so they partake of a 'post-post-modern' return to
sources, or, more simply put, a reconsideration of modernism's
unfinished business, of which the idea of animating what was once
inanimate is a primary part, and the technical possibility of slowing it
down or holding it as still as paintings or sculptures are the obvious
corollaries. Like the self-portrait image in *Bear*, McQueen is poised to
spring at us – and will – but in waiting for his moment, he stares down
the camera, lets time run against the near rigidity of his stance, and
makes us see, as we have rarely seen before, the tension between
temporal flow and obdurate self-containment, the perceptual break
between images that move automatically and things in the world that
may or may not. And like the similarly frozen self-portrait image in
Deadpan, McQueen is in complete charge of whether they do or don't.

Just Above My Head, 1996

MCQUEEN'S MATERIALISM

Michael Newman

Steve McQueen's approach shows a tendency towards structural inversion, both within works and between them, which is an indication of his concern with form. Without reducing the importance of questions of content, it is necessary to see how these are worked through in formal transformations, before throwing into question the very distinction between form and content. Notice in *Bear* and *Five Easy Pieces* the contrast between horizontal and vertical, near and distant: the interest is in *relations between shots and bodies*, both those on screen and that of the spectator off screen. *Just Above My Head* and *Deadpan* make a pair in terms of movement and stasis, framing and unframing in films that involve a *performance* by the artist. *Catch* and *Drumroll* form a set with *White Elephant*, despite their different media. In all three there is a step-by-step archaeological turning inside-out of cinematic representation, since they are all concerned with the *apparatus*. The development is from cinema, through performance, to sculpture. The end is already implicit since from the start cinema is reinscribed as installation, reinterpreted in such a way that film becomes a performative and sculptural medium. These displacements open up the possibility of engaging a political history of media where, through a rigorously formal approach form is exceeded.

Displacements

In *Bear* (1993) McQueen and another black man, both naked, circle around each other, moving between aggression and desire. At the beginning there is a use of 'flare' as the heads move across lights towards which the slightly raised camera points. This has a transfiguring effect on the bodies, reminiscent of the fight scenes in *Raging Bull*. In another sequence a crouching McQueen charges towards his opponent. The final reverse shot, which in Hollywood would show the consequence of the action, is left showing barely a flailing limb, as if to suggest that the attempt to catch the other ends with nothing, or with the loss of the desired. The final sequences are reminiscent of the wrestling episode in Ken Russell's *Women in Love*.[1] Two features can be noted here. First, the view of the genitals from below bespeaks vulnerability rather than macho aggression. Second, in the final sequence of legs and feet, there is a dance-like springiness to the steps. This is the result of editing the film in such a way that this sequence plays backwards. As in those earlier moments, when the film is slowed and sped up, attention is drawn to the usually forgotten temporality of film, and, beyond that, to the time of desire and loss, as a corollary to the movements of pursuit and evasion.

Here we have the portrayal of an intimate exchange between two men to which a number of codes from cinema apply. Ambivalence appears at two levels: the first is between desire and aggression; the second is in relation to form. On the one hand, the formal dimension - particularly in the use of lighting and camera angles - is stressed as transfiguration. On the other, it comes close to parody, an emptying out of meaning and a foregrounding of given codes. The result is an oscillation between the representation of emotion and the stereotypical modes that make it possible. A stereotype is repeated - the black male's prowess at fighting - to be undermined, both *as* repetition and as displacement into the representation of love and vulnerability. McQueen does not content himself with appropriation or stereotype, he rather directs his attention to the *refunctioning* of form. There is a tension here, too, since 'displacement' suggests ambivalence as analysed by Homi Bhabha in describing the reception of the English book in a colonial setting. He writes, "such an image can neither be 'original' - by virtue of the act of repetition that constructs it - nor 'identical' - by virtue of the difference that defines it."[2] In McQueen's film-installation the tension arises in the relation between the deconstructive repetition and the 'constructive' refunctioning. By contrast with the earlier avant-garde, the refunctioning serves not use-value so much as intensification. McQueen has said:

> Projecting the film on to the back wall of the gallery space so that it completely fills it from ceiling to floor, and from side to side, gives it this kind of blanket effect. You are very much involved with what is going on... The whole idea of making it a silent experience is so that when people walk into the space they become very much aware of themselves, of their own breathing... I find it difficult to breathe when I'm in the space... I want to put people into a situation where they're sensitive to themselves watching the piece.[3]

I want to stress the tension between the repetition of codes and the intensification of a self-conscious bodily experience. It demonstrates the dilemma of critique: how to reinstate experience without recourse to a criterion of authenticity that depends on the dominant culture that is being critiqued.

What is striking is the evocation of distance: if *Bear* tries to bridge a gap on a horizontal axis - the bodies move around, towards and away - *Five Easy Pieces* interposes a distance on an up-down axis. If *Bear* recalls Hollywood's treatment of the intimate life of the body, *Five Easy Pieces* recalls the look of Constructivist avant-garde photography. The initial axis established is the one between the shots up, towards the female tightrope walker, and down, towards the five male hula-hoopers. Both the cruciform of the shoulders of the woman, and the circles and shadows of the men, recall Constructivist photography, especially the late 1920s photographs of Rodchenko. That the cuts are between different scenarios rather than, as in *Bear*, counter-shots within the same scene, gives this film as a whole a more 'constructed' feel. Changes in the rhythm of cuts, and rhythmic movement within shots, tend towards a more musical sense of structure, although the film is silent. It feels more like an autonomous temporal-sculptural work, and less like an episode from a film. If that were all, we could say that Constructivism is recuperated as style for autonomous art. But it is not all. First, all the subjects are black, which introduces otherness into the earlier avant-garde's claim to universality. Second, linked with this, there are two 'actions' - each divided in two - that disrupt the reading in terms of style. One is the scene in which the artist is shot from below taking his penis from his pants and pissing down towards the camera/viewer. This was achieved by pissing into a glass container above the camera, the effect is for a moment to render the screen opaque and to abject the viewer.

The second disruptive action involves two shots in extreme close-up moving around a black man's face - which we might suppose is the artist's - with an endoscope. The first sequence focuses on the lips, the second on the eyes and nostrils. That these are in colour, and in a very grainy video quite different from the smooth monochrome perfection of the 16mm sequences, makes them all the more startling. These shots seem to do two things: first, they break through visual distance by introducing a mode of filming that is almost tactile, close, textured and with an extreme reduction of spatial markers for orientation. The other aspect links it to the pissing sequence: in the latter, the object of the gaze 'hits' the eye of the viewer. In the former, the camera almost hits the face of the 'object', fragmenting the man's lips, eyes, nostrils. In both cases this 'in your face' gesture achieves a kind of reversal between subject and object, where the camera collides with the object of the gaze to become an eye looking out at the viewer. [4] This drive to take film beyond film allies McQueen's approach with the film and video performance art of the 1970s, which this work sets in relation with Constructivist camerawork. What keeps an image in its place is the way it is framed, physically and institutionally. Installation is essential to McQueen's work of unframing, while its opposite - in freeing the image and restoring presence it installs it all the more auratically in place - is experienced as suffocation.

Framing and Unframing

Just Above My Head is a 9 minutes, 35 seconds single take of a white, cloudy sky with the artist's head bobbing at the bottom of the frame as he walks. His pace is determined - more a march than a stroll - as his head slips in and out of the frame. While being closer to performance art than the previous films - an economical single action - it also depends on the framing of the image. It suggests a relation between film and performance comparable with early films by Acconci, which attempt to negotiate an immediate relation with the viewer, as well as those of Warhol, where a single action, such as eating a mushroom or being fellated off screen, is filmed in real time. Like all McQueen's films, *Just Above My Head* is projected as an installation, filling a wall from floor to ceiling. This shifts the experience of the viewer from that of being a pure look, to being an embodied subject. The lower edge of the image is placed at floor level, so that the head appears to be trying to keep itself afloat, an effect stressed further when the floor reflects the image. A narrative element is provided by the branches of the trees that appear at the end, like a life-raft.[5] If to be incorporated is suffocating, to be excluded is obliterating.

It is possible to think of the out-of-frame as allegorising exclusion in a political sense. The figure-ground relations are traditionally keyed to frame a white face. This is so almost from the start in the 1890s Kinetoscope films of Edison's associate W.K.L. Dickson, where a black backdrop was used to centre the scene and render it intelligible - presupposing white faces. Noël Burch sees this establishment of a centripetal, figure-ground image as a foreclosure of the decentred possibilities of Lumière's early films.[6] The head of a black person pushing into a light sky from the surrounding darkness will appear quite differently from a white head, either in the same circumstance, or against a dark background. This draws attention to the exclusions involved in the formal history of the medium. The light levels of Hollywood cinema are set for the norm of white skin, which means black actors have to be very strongly lit to compensate. By contrast, we can now see that McQueen's earlier films have been lit for black skin, creating a quite different tone. We can also see how different McQueen's reference to framing is from a purely structural approach. He gives a hint of what cinema might have been had it included black subjects as central to its project. Political ramifications do not stop at the level of content. A materialist analysis of form would show how its apparent contingencies are overdetermined.

Whereas in *Just Above My Head* McQueen is in motion, in *Deadpan* he is still. Whereas in the former the figure intrudes from outside the

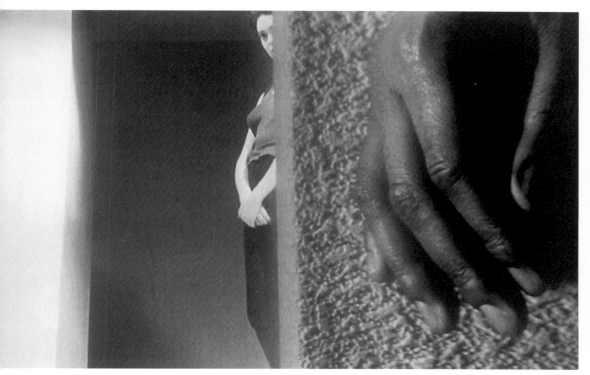

Stage, 1996

frame, in the latter the frame falls around a centred figure. Indeed, it is almost as if, whereas the artist is trying to break into the frame in *Just Above My Head*, he *is* the screen in *Deadpan*, an impassive surface for the projection of narrative and fantasy. As the wall of the A-frame house falls forward, the artist is literally 'framed' by the window frame, while the film itself is framed by its means. The first shot is from inside the building, beginning when the fall of the wall lets in light; the last shot is of the wall falling onto the camera, and ends in darkness. The shots in between analyse the gag from all points of view: feet from the front (shoelaces missing); centred on the window, which reveals the interior of the building when it falls; the window to the left, with the camera following the movement of the falling wall ending with McQueen's legs; the artist's body in an 'American shot' cut above the legs; a side view of the upper torso as the wall passes; a downward shot from the upper window rapidly repeated; a frontal shot of the window cut by the frame; oscillating still-shots of the face; and the face with the wall falling across it. The tension of this work derives from two contradictory effects of the repetition. On the one hand, a tendency towards an abstracting normalisation; on the other, the repetition turns the gag into an ordeal that the artist must undergo without even blinking an eye. The middle of the film is punctuated by a sequence where the artist's face is shown in an oscillation of still-shots before and after the fall of the wall, the alteration in lighting creating an illusion of movement.

What is at issue here is the relation of the gag to its formal effect when it is removed from the causality of a plot narrative. Attention is shifted from the narrative of plot, as in *Steamboat Bill Jr*, to the way an event or story is constructed in the plasticity of its signifiers. However, the Brechtian detachment of an earlier avant-garde cannot simply be repeated. In an epoch where such disengagement has become the norm, the foregrounding of the signifier needs some kind of counter-engagement that does not re-fetishize the object.

While in the source of the gag, the 1928 silent comedy *Steamboat Bill Jr*, Buster Keaton is in movement, running through the windstorm, McQueen is motionless. Whereas the actions in *Steamboat Bill Jr* are causally motivated, the repetition of the gag in *Deadpan* eliminates causality. This leaves the gag open for reinscription: by withholding a plot, it invites interpretation by the viewer. Interpretations in terms of race are possible, yet any determinate meaning remains suspended in the impassivity of the figure. *Deadpan* suggests various frames in order to unframe itself. The narrative of its source is displaced by the formal presence of the abstract shots, but the formal, 'painterly' reading in turn is blocked by rhythm, above all by the oscillating interpellation of

Catch, 1997

the stills. McQueen incorporates the repetition implicit in its mode of presentation in the structure of the film. The installation encourages repeated viewings - the viewer can come and go at any time - while going against it through the emphatic opening and closing of the sequence of shots. Both the use of repetition and the film's relation to its viewing conditions distinguish it from classic cinema. The different shots of the repeated action create a double ambiguity. First, are we watching a continuum - the marked beginning and ending implies this - or the same action from different perspectives? And second, are we watching a documentary or documentation of a performance, or a series of retakes towards a fictional construction, like the source-movie?[7] The question of truth intersects with that of time: does the repetition-with-difference verify the truth of the event or heighten its conventionality, and does it intensify or subvent presence?

The same repetition that enables formal abstraction opens the film to a deformalising rhythm. The 'flicker' effect emphasises the materiality of the image and produces a syncope in the narrative: repetition gives way to interruption. Rosalind Krauss writes of Duchamp's *Anémic Cinéma* (1925) with Man Ray, and the *Rotoreliefs* (1935): "the throb of his revolving disks, pulsing as they do with erotic suggestiveness, opens the very concept of visual autonomy - of a form of experience that is wholly and purely optical, owing nothing to time - to the invasion of a sense of dense, corporeal pressure."[8] She extends this deformalising project to Nauman's *Lip Synch* (1969) and Serra's *Hand Catching Lead* (1971), associating the latter with the 'flicker film'[9] in a way that suggests a genealogy for McQueen's work. Consider also the relation between repetition and trauma: *Deadpan* - the 180-degree pan ends in extinction - could be perceived as a recurring dream of a traumatic event. Its 'form' acquires the character of compulsion, attempting to capture an experience that was missed, condensed into the before-and-after stills of the 'flicker' sequence, which collapses the viewer's physical distance from the image like a strobe-light.[10]

According to Walter Benjamin, what a phenomenon essentially is - what it might have been - flares up at the moment of its disappearance. It is not surprising that artists have turned to film at a time when the classic institutional mode of cinema is coming to an end and when its ageing is an essential aspect of their experience. In its obsolescence film becomes available as a medium for visual art. It seems that McQueen 'reads' film through the performance-based film and video art of the late 60s and early 70s (Warhol, Nauman, Acconci, Serra, Graham), which provides a more physical and pragmatic interpretation compared to the language-based structuralist approach. *Deadpan* could evoke a Chris Burden action, such as *Shoot* (1971) where the artist stood still to be shot in the arm. This effects a belated reinscription of film beyond its dominant institutional mode, with the centred viewer-subject and narrative closure. We might think back, not only to the great gag comedies of silent film, but earlier, to cinema as fairground spectacle, recalled in McQueen's presentation of his films as installations, rather than in an auditorium with seats riveting the spectator. Instead of simply using avant-garde techniques within the film, while the audience remains stationary, McQueen displaces cinema into a set-up in which the viewers are made physically aware of their relation to the screen. This restores the 'external relation'[11] to the film - consciously watching pictures unfold on a screen in front of one - that preceded the interpellation of the spectator-subject in the classic cinema from the second decade of the century. Hence the reference to a moment when film itself was a performance art, in a way quite different to that of theatre - perhaps closer to the circus.

Reflecting Medium

In this sense the sculpture-installation *White Elephant* (1998) is consistent with the film-installations, and follows logically from *Catch* (1997) and *Drumroll* (1998). *Catch* deconstructs the classic structure of shot and counter-shot, where the viewer is constructed through identification, an effect usually reinforced by dialogue. In *Catch* the alternation between portrait-shots of the artist and his sister, both wearing bright and clashing clothes, is conducted in silence, with expressionless faces in order to block identification. The 'deconstruction' consists in not turning off the camera between what would normally be distinct shots. Like *Just Above My Head* it is one continuous, unedited shoot. The camera is thrown between the two like a ball.

At this point we may recall three moments from Antonioni's film *The Passenger*. The first is when Locke (Jack Nicholson), a reporter trying to make a documentary on a rebellion in central Africa who has taken over the identity of a dead gun-runner, is shown in earlier footage interviewing a 'witch doctor', who takes revenge for Locke's condescension by turning the camera on him.[12] The African thus becomes the subject and the white reporter the object of the look. The second is during an interview with an African ruler, when the camera makes a 360-degree pan, showing troops and police, who belie his claim that 'there is no opposition'. The political is implicit in the structure of the shot, rather than simply in the content of what is said, as is also the case in all McQueen's film-installations, most hieratically in *Deadpan* and *Catch*. The third moment is the extraordinary long loop the camera makes towards the end of the film, during which Locke's death, which is not shown, takes place. Here the camera detaches itself from the viewpoint of any possible subject. In this way a formal device reveals the alterity of the filmic image, which takes on a materiality in its independence from subjective consciousness.

The effect of the game of *Catch* is that the camera is shown in the process of separating itself from subjective points of view, which equally breaks the identification of the spectator with the camera, which is exploited in the close-up shot an counter-shot of classic cinema. Already in *Deadpan* the conditions of the representation have become part of the content. Now it is as if that which produces the image is taking on a life of its own. This move reminds one of Dan Graham's *Body Press* (1970-72) where a naked man and woman pass video-cameras around their bodies, although unlike *Catch* the latter is not indebted to the codes of cinema, but concerned in a more 'phenomenological' way with the break between bodily experience and representation.[13] None the less the action of *Catch* draws on the work of the 70s in that it breaks through representation via performance into what is perhaps best called sculpture.[14]

This externalisation of the body with respect to the camera is extended in *Drumroll*, where three video cameras are placed in an oil drum, one filming through each end, and one through a hole in the side. This is the first of the works to use sound, the ambient sound of the action, such as the artist saying "sorry, sorry, sorry" as he rolls the drum along three streets in midtown Manhattan. Like Robert Morris's *Box With the Sound of Its Own Making* (1961), it is a work that records its own construction, while subverting any contemplative fetishization. The three videos thus produced are projected onto screens forming a triptych, referring simultaneously to performance, sculpture and painting. Not to assimilate these traditions, but to explore their contradictions and tensions in order to find a place for a critical practice. On one side, shop windows and avenues; on the other, parked cars, the road and traffic, and in the centre the artist in pink coat and jeans, the sky, and the ground which punctuates this sequence with black. The effect of watching these different rotations simultaneously is a nauseating dizziness. The 'motionless voyage' of classic cinema, which constitutes the ubiquitous, disembodied subject,[15] becomes a bumpy ride in which the viewer is at once internal to the action by identification with the camera, and external through the triptych structure. We can neither take the position of any of the cameras, nor can we take the position of the artist who rolls the drum, since from moment to moment we are looking at him from the inside. We are his victims as it were.

By contrast with the hieratic centring of the image, which we see in *Deadpan* and in the portrait poses of *Catch*, here there is an extreme

Deadpan, 1997

decentring of the camera from any possible subject position. That
reminds us of those moments in early film, before the camera assumed
its identity with the point of view of subjective consciousness, through
multiplication, and through the creation of what is in effect a machine
to produce the image. The contingency of this machine subverts the
God-like viewpoint of that other extension of street photography, CCTV.
Projected as a triptych, *Drumroll* actually creates two temporalities: the
flow of the side cameras contrasts with the central projection, which
pulses black as the camera points downwards. The rhythm of all of
them varies and sometimes almost comes to a stop as the artist meets
an obstruction. Compare this with the interposition of the rhythmic
flicker in *Deadpan*, the alternation of portrait shots and throws in *Catch*
and the endoscope sequences in *Five Easy Pieces*. To which we can add
the rhythm of the hand that dives down and pulls back in *Something
old, Something new, Something borrowed, Something blue*, (1998) a
two-minute film-loop edited from *Stage* (1996) and projected down,
towards the floor. If the Hollywood norm of cinema is for film to be
identified with the continuous flow of life - although it is editing that
makes this illusion possible - here a suppressed pulse breaks through.

It is generally thought that film emerged out of a number of different
kinds of optical instruments and toys, rotated by hand, with slits
through which, by superimposition, the image flickered into movement.
One of these was the Praxinoscope, patented in 1877, where rectangular
mirrors set around an inner drum reflected images on a strip set on the
inside of an outer wall. Viewed through a square aperture, surrounded
by a painting of a proscenium arch, these images sprang into movement
as the drum was rotated.[16] McQueen's installation *White Elephant* (1998)
is in effect the central drum of the Praxinoscope, enlarged and turned
into a playground roundabout, the mirror-effect imitated by the chrome,
reflecting, instead of the image on the perimeter, the visitors to the
gallery. The walls of the room are painted a warm kitsch pink,
contrasting with the cold chrome of the reflecting machine and
suggesting the colour of a child's room. This continues the trajectory of
Catch and *Drumroll*, in that the installation is just the image-producing
mechanism, rather than the presentation of a representation resulting
from it. With this work McQueen's 'archaeology of the cinema' is
completed, as sculpture. There is something here of the adapted ready-
made - recall Duchamp's interest in optical instruments, and the history
of 'reflective' works of art, such as Rauschenberg's *White Paintings*
(1951) and more obviously the mirror paintings with images of people -
such as anti-Vietnam war demonstrators - stuck to them, made by
Pistoletto from 1962.[17] But *White Elephant* is not simply a return to a

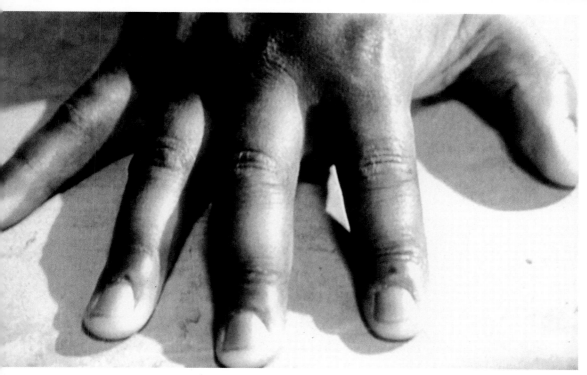

Something old, Something new, Somehing borrowed, Something blue, 1998

precursor. Nor is it an acquiescence in the 'disciplinary' effect of mid-nineteenth-century optical machines.[18] The body is simultaneously captivated - consider *Deadpan* - and released (recall Dan Graham's time-delay video and two way mirror installations[19]). Viewers and spectacle become one, not in the apotheosis of the image or pure simulation, but rather, with an internal separation between the mobile, active body and its reflection. Through his excavation of suppressed possibility in the material history of a medium, facilitated by displacements between film, sculpture, performance and installation, and by a rigorous work on form in production and presentation, Steve McQueen suggests how things could still work out differently.

NOTES

This text has been immeasurably improved thanks to the help and advice of Rebecca Comay.

1. This is suggested by both David A. Bailey (*Mirage: Enigmas of Race, Difference and Desire*, London, ICA and InIVA, 1995, p.64) and Jon Thompson ("'It's the Way You Tell'em': Narrative Cliché in the Films of Steve McQueen" in *Steve McQueen*, Frankfurt am Main, Portikus and Eindhoven, Stedelijk Van Abbemuseum, 1997, p.7).

2. Homi K. Bhabha, "Signs Taken for Wonders: Questions of Ambivalence and Authority under a Tree Outside Delhi, May 1817" in Henry Louis Gates, Jr. ed., *'Race', Writing and Difference*, Chicago and London, University of Chicago Press, 1986, p.169.

3. "Let's Get Physical: Steve McQueen interviewed by Patricia Bickers", *Art Monthly*, No.202, Dec. 1996-Jan. 1997, p.2.

4. Compare this with the use of the endoscope in Mona Hatoum's video-installation *Corps étrangers* (1994).

5. Jon Thompson compares this to a moment from Robert Bresson's *Diary of a Country Priest* (*op.cit.*, p.9).

6. Noël Burch, *Life to those Shadows*, London, BFI, 1990, pp.30-4.

7. See Peter Gidal, *Materialist Film*, London, Routledge, 1989, pp.22-4. My discussion should have indicated how McQueen continues to develop certain issues from structural-materialist film of the late 60s and 70s. For this background, see also Malcolm LeGrice, *Abstract Film and Beyond*, London, Studio Vista, 1977.

8. Yve-Alain Bois and Rosalind E. Krauss, *Formless: A User's Guide*, New York, Zone Books, 1997, p.135.

9. "A genre characterised by its use of rapidly alternating black and white frames, and seeking both to develop an 'abstract' film idiom and to harken back to the beginning days of cinema, when the primitive technology of the medium caused the image to jerk or 'flicker'. *Ibid.*, p.136.

10. See Krauss on James Coleman's *Box (ahhareturnabout)*, (1977) in *Formless*, pp.161-5.

11. See Seymour Chatman, *Antonioni; or, The Surface of the World*, Berkeley, University of California Press, 1985, pp. 182-202.

12. Burch, *op.cit.*, p.204.

13. There is a small illustration of this work in the catalogue *Acting Out. The Body in Video: Then and Now*, curated by Julia Bunnage *et al.*, Royal College of Art, 1994, an exhibition which featured Steve McQueen's *Bear*.

14. In conversation with the author Steve McQueen repeatedly referred to his works, including those using film and video, as 'sculpture" (Amsterdam, 9 December 1998).

15. See Burch, pp.202-30.

16. See C.W. Ceran, *Archaeology of the Cinema*, London, Thames and Hudson, 1965, figs.80-84.

17. Tony Godfrey writes: "These were elegant works, but ones which problematized the position of the viewer: as Ad Reinhardt would have said, the question was not what the painting represented, but what you represented." *Conceptual Art*, London, Phaidon, 1998, p.114.

18. See Jonathan Crary, *Techniques of the Observer: On Vision and Modernity in the Nineteenth Century*, Cambridge, Mass., The MIT Press, 1992, pp.129-32. Crary questions the account of mid-nineteenth-century optical instruments as precursors to film, seeing them rather in terms of a distinctive discourse of vision involving the eradication of the 'point of view' (p.128), and the location of vision in terms of physiological quantities, dissolving the boundary between subjective interiority and the world.

19. For Dan Graham's turn to themes of childhood and play, see *Children's Pavilion* (with Jeff Wall), and *Skateboard Pavilion*, both 1989.

HAPTIC VISIONS
THE FILMS OF STEVE McQUEEN

Okwui Enwezor

The visual is essentially pornographic, which is to say that it has its end in rapt, mindless fascination; thinking about its attributes becomes an adjunct to that, if it is unwilling to betray its object; while the most austere films necessarily draw their energy from the attempt to repress their own excess (rather than from the thankless effort to discipline the viewer). Pornographic films are thus only the potentiation of films in general, which asks us to stare at the world as though it were a naked body.

Fredric Jameson "Introduction" in *Signatures of the Visible*

I

*F*ew young artists have so convincingly entered their work into the public sphere with so emphatic a purpose and concentration as Steve McQueen did with his highly praised and now classic first film *Bear* (1993), in London at the Royal College of Art in 1994. Though *Bear* is generally described as a highly formal film, its critical intelligence, toughness and elegance posited the bare fact that a compelling and arresting work is possible with only the rudimentary elements of film language, without recourse to over-rehearsed pyrotechnic visual effect. For McQueen, to make art with film, one had to first wrestle with the imposing legacy of the history of cinema. Cinema in all its variety, from classical genre films of early Hollywood (*film noir*, musicals, comedy, westerns) to the experimental work of independent productions (art house), artists' films (structural films and early video), pornographic films and documentary work. Approached with such sharp focus, and faithful to the well-worn craft of cinema as a signifying artistic tool, the defining character of all of McQueen's work privileges enunciation over style, legibility over maudlin theatrics. Film has to be made transparent to the viewer in a stripped down fashion that takes the filmic form to its basic structural elements in order to then repossess the vitality of its language. This approach has resulted in a group of now nine films, so crisp and uncluttered that the cinematic form has acquired both a sensuous clarity and mysteriousness not often seen in video or film work by artists working today.

As much as being part of the fundamental progression of avant-garde cinema and films by artists since the 1960s and an heir to its many theoretical concerns with the image, on the surface, the hallmarks of, and the conditions that characterise Steve McQueen's film-installations seem to rebut Fredric Jameson's assertion. His assertion may be true for the popular genre of film-as-spectacle and entertainment; a numbing event whose technologies of fascination turn the world into a pulsing, throbbing body to be stared at and consumed. However, at the opposite end of the spectrum of this generally accepted theory, in which viewers are willing to be absorbed and swallowed by the seduction of the silver screen, are works by artists that utilise the technology of film, but work in a way that is different from the conventional strategy of film-as-spectacle and entertainment. One early example of the avant-garde's contestation of the status of the filmic image and cinema is Guy Debord's *Hurlements* from the late 1950s, which consists entirely of the oscillation between flickering empty black and white screens; in other words an *imageless* film. The works of Michael Snow from the early 60s, in which not much is seen to happen, and in which all the traditional conventions of narrative structure are dismantled, are another example. Bruce Nauman is one of the artists, who - in his early work - challenged the notion that film, at least when made with the gallery space in mind, was mostly concerned with the form of the naked body.

Steve McQueen falls into the category of artists who work with the language of film, but are neither interested in its conventional narrative structure, nor in replicating the same conditions of scopic abduction of the viewer into the seedy abyss of the pornographic, which popular cinema is seen to propose. McQueen's works, like those of Debord, Snow, and Nauman, start with the intention of breaking down the given gospel of Jameson's assertion of the essential pornographic nature of the visual. His film-installations explore the relationship between the medium and the viewer as active and mutually interpolated and mediating forces of the viewing experience. By making the conditions under which the projected film image is experienced both visually and bodily, McQueen renders the space of cinema into a zone that is simultaneously haptic and optical. The overwhelming physicality and raw immediacy of the encounter between the viewing subject and the films, reinforce the haptic/optical scope. This makes the necessary differentiation between cinema as theatre and film as an embodied, artistic gesture.

2

How precisely may we analyse McQueen's film-installations as simultaneously haptic and optical? Let's begin with the conventional description of the films, which, quite correctly, have been identified as black and white, silent films. Are they silent films or are they films without sound? This seems a rather technical argument. However, if we say the films are silent, we have to make them respond to the conditions of early cinema; these films are silent because of the inability at the time to synchronise moving image with sound. Early silent films however, were often accompanied by a piano player, which of course rendered them not silent at all. If, on the other hand, we say that McQueen's films are silent, we have to assume a conscious decision not to have an extraneous sound that might impose an unwarranted narrative on his films. Therefore, the fact that his films are silent is based on a critical artistic decision, rather than one of technological impossibility. Consequently, it would be correct to say that McQueen's films, in the conventional sense of understanding the difference between early silent films and early talkies, are not silent films at all. They are consciously *drained* of sound. This interest to drain the image of sound - either by not recording it, or by erasing afterwards - is related to the haptic characterisation I put forward as one way the installations are being experienced.

From the moment the viewer enters his film-installations, there is a feeling of spatial dislocation and contraction that turns the social dynamics of the cinematic space into that of a decentred ambient zone; one that is proportionate to the sensory adjustments of the body's physical properties. It is an experience that is at once psychic and physical. The encounter with the projected image renders the spectator into a dialogue, into a transtextual, relational correspondence. The breathing of the viewer and his physical awareness of the room and the nearness of the image that fills one section of its walls, provides the kind of rich sensory synapses that makes the entire room seem to shudder with sound. In *Bear*, for example, one suspects it is not the 'actual' sound of the struggling bodies of the two nude men wrestling that constitutes the 'real' sound of the film. Rather, the viewer's reception or physical experience of the men's two bodies touching, foregrounds the sound. It is thus in vain that we demand of McQueen's films a 'natural' sound of the actions in order to allow us to complete the narrative linearity we may wish to impose upon them.

One way the effortless physicality of the projected image is accomplished is by treating the image as if it were a kind of object. Another way in which the projected image seems alternately physical and illusionistic is that it is dependent upon very clearly specified conditions. On the physical level there are the intentional graininess of the black and white film, the close-ups of the body parts, jerky movement of the camera, the spinning, whirling movement of the figures in the films, the *chiaroscuro* achieved through lighting and the editing format (slow and fast motion). Then there are the actual specifications of the room, which usually measures 6 x 4 x 3 metres (length, width, and height). In these very carefully constructed conditions, the image is projected floor to ceiling, wall to wall, to a kind of monumentality that is totally un-spectacular. There is little space to avoid the impact and looming centrality of the image. We are invited into what ostensibly is a box, instead of into a cavernous, lush movie theatre, which means the viewer has to go through a process of adjustment once inside the specially constructed room.

This process of adjustment equally calls to the viewer's attention of the sculptural physicality of the image. The overwhelming proximity to the performing body in the film seems to involve the viewer in the camera's actions, but in a way that neither fetishises the body nor the apparatus. Proximity is further accentuated by the absence of chairs, and because the viewer has to stand to watch and engage in the image, there is always a relational correspondence between the filmic body and the physical body.

3

One other way to discuss these films is through their relationship to realism. Nowhere is realism deployed more to its full hallucinatory effect than in *Bear* and *Five Easy Pieces* (1995). In *Bear* the stop-motion effect of the two struggling bodies composes them into alternately fragmented and restored wholes. The camera's actions consistently remain focused, not so much on the bodies of the men, but on the space of the action, which is the space of the film. Even when the bodies tumble and collapse on the floor or vanish from view, the awareness of the screen that configures their corporeality remains intact. When we are watching the film, it suddenly becomes clear that we are not so much observing the two fighting bodies as much as following the camera's lens. There is an amazing circularity performed and achieved by the camera, and one is essentially left breathless in admiration of McQueen's directorial prowess. This circularity is not achieved through panning though, but by the continuous adjustments the camera makes to the movement of the actors. In each portion and segment of the film the camera's angle, position and distance determines the place of the viewer, vis-à-vis the body. *Bear* reminds me not only of Eadweard Muybridge's stop-motion photographs, but also of the incredibly restrained light and control of Roy Decarava's black and white photographs, and Alexander Rodchenko's photographs of the 1920s and 30s.

Five Easy Pieces does what *Bear* does, but instead of focusing on one continuous take of an action, it bisects the cinematic space into vertical, horizontal and diagonal bands. The manner in which space is organised, the placement of the performing figures in perfectly

White Elephant, 1998

symetrical formations, the play between light and shadow, right and left angles, vertical to horizontal axis, are techniques that again recall Decarava and Rodchenko's use of vertical angles, by photographing the subject from above or below.[1] Again, when watching the action of the film, we may suppose we are watching the performers, which of course, indeed, we are. But by following the movement of the figures, the viewer is able to deduce that, in essence, he is also watching the camera, as it defines the spaces as seen from below, either with the tight rope walker, slithering and balancing atop the rope, or the man pissing into the camera and on us. Notice in the figures of the five hula-hooping men and their shadows - again seen from above - the circularity of the camera, a trademark of Decarava (*Five Figures on a Harlem Street*, shot from above) and Rodchenko (*Sucharev Tower*, shot from below). These are not just formal exercises. In each film, the sense of effortless grace that he achieves is based precisely on the fact that McQueen's interest is in finding a way to allow the camera to make a compelling story without overly scripting the outcome. That he succeeds time and again, is testament to his profound understanding of the plastic possibilities of film.

4

It is in the plastic possibilities of film that McQueen attempts to both deploy and subvert realism. For him realism is the theatre in which cinema breaks with the tradition of pure documentary film. As the imaginative realm which interposes fiction and fantasy with the real, it recreates the symbiosis between the self and the other. Gilles Deleuze has discussed realism as located and "actualised directly in determinate, geographical, historical, social space-time".[2] Deleuze also proposed one element of realism as constituting an embodiment in "behaviour, in the form of emotions or passions which order or disorder it".[3]

One thing the viewer is constantly made aware of while watching any of McQueen's films, is the space-time dimension. If realism requires, according to Deleuze, certain types of embodiment in historical, geographical, social, and even perhaps cultural space-time, McQueen found at least one crucial solution for his installations, by having the floor of the gallery polished to a shiny reflective surface, which literally doubles the projected image like a mirror. There is obviously nothing radical about this kind of perspectival device that painters have utilised for centuries, and that was most recently used to such incredible effectiveness by the German painter Gerhard Richter. The importance then, of the device of the reflective floor is essential to the understanding of his overall critical strategy, which becomes obvious

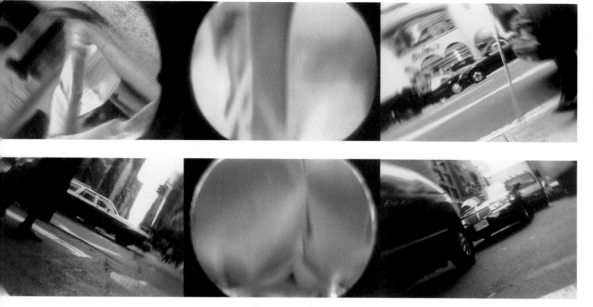

Drumroll, 1998

when one enters his installations. Not only is the film reflected on the floor, the viewer's own reflection is incorporated into the reflection. Thus, the viewer is not only physically subsumed into the space-time of the installation, but illusionistically inserted and merged into it. McQueen's films seriously propose that there are at least two ways of 'seeing' his work; one through the conventional optical mode of simply watching the image, and the other by 'physically' (haptically) seeing the film through the body, as illusionistic sensations.

5

A consistent and recurring analysis of McQueen's films is that they are generally about nothing, or seem to be about nothing, at least in the classic language of structuralist films of the 1960s, which privilege process over any ascertainable narrative linearity. This sense of nothingness, could be explored as one way in which formal criticism sets up its own internal logic, while assiduously avoiding other tracking devices that may allow for more complex, and less opportunistic elaborations, which could lead to other conclusions. However, the purported contentlessness of McQueen's work, is neither a drive towards an inchoate mystery, nor is it the non-place of representation into which viewers are invited to fill the blank spaces.

Far from it, all of McQueen's films do possess clear, legible programmes. In an interview, McQueen gave as one of the reasons why he left film school in New York his disappointment with what he thought film school should be; the very emblem of experimentation. For him it was the opposite, literally suffocating, "they wouldn't let you throw the camera up in the air and catch it." *Catch* (1997) first screened at *Documenta X* in Kassel, was clearly a response to his frustrations and short lived residence in film school. The film comprises alternating shots of McQueen and his sister tossing a camera back and forth to each other, as if to illustrate the point that there are no limits to what can be done with the camera. That the action takes place on a patch of green, in a field where McQueen and his sister played as little children, might indeed be suggestive of other, less certain motives for the film. That suddenly, the film we've all come to see as an occasion of an artist extending his dramatic and filmic range, is given a new powerful and ambiguous narrative tension, indicates how easily we misread his work. McQueen was well aware that *Catch*, would not be the wonderful film it is, by simply showing up his former professors. It was clearly an impetus in the making of the film. Like all his previous work, which seems to have indecipherable and cryptic codes within them, *Catch* ultimately finds a way to elude easy categorisation.

Exodus (1992/97) might be McQueen's concession to an overtly precise narrative. The short colour film (65 seconds) is one continuous shot of two west-Indian men, carrying two potted palms through a busy London street. The two well-dressed figures weave their way through the throng until they cross the street and board their bus and wave. *Exodus* maps into a kind of subtle diasporic consciousness-raising. It pits the elegant cosmopolitan ideal of two well-dressed black men sauntering down the streets of a major city, with Bob Marley's rousing reggae anthem of departure from Babylon and return to the promised land. McQueen's quotation of the biblical ethos of Marley's popular narrative of dislocation and return seen in the context of Britain's west-Indian immigrants, is both humorous and ironic.

Even a film like *Just Above My Head*, which essentially is one take of the one action of McQueen striding towards the camera, may seem contentless if the plethora of associations that shadow it are not carefully attended to. In the film, most of McQueen's body is literally cropped off, leaving only his head bouncing off of the polished floor like the severed head of John the Baptist on a platter or like the lugubrious heads of Symbolist painter Odilon Redon. Behind the striding figure, an immense white space looms, filling the distance, making the installation space into a ponderous white screen; a disturbing and enervating presence. When the figure finally emerges, towards the end of the film, in a landscape with trees, it becomes quite clear that this is a precisely scripted work, albeit with a highly distilled narrative.

Several references immediately jump to mind: the first one, to James Baldwin's novel *Just Above My Head*, is an obvious nod to black literary and intellectual presentness. The second, Toni Morrison's brilliant discussion of literary whiteness in an American literature intent on subduing a figurative Africanist presence in novels such as Melville's *Moby Dick* and Edgar Allan Poe's *The Narrative of Arthur Gordon Pym*, provides another crucial source for a productive reading of the film. In her book *Playing in the Dark: Whiteness and the Literary Imagination* (1992) Morrison writes that the "images of impenetrable whiteness need contextualizing to explain their extraordinary power, pattern and consistency." At the other end of the spectrum, much earlier than Morrison, Zola Neale Hurston would write in an essay in the 1920s that she feels most black when thrown against a sharp white background. What we are hearing here are meditations on the contradictory impressions of whiteness as both anathema and accompaniment to this figurative, black, Africanist presence.

McQueen himself puts the issue in these terms in an interview when discussing *Just Above My Head*: "For me that whole thing was to do with gravity. All along, all you've seen is empty sky, just *whiteness* (my emphasis) with this head bobbing along. Then we see these tree branches spread across the screen and its like 'Oh we've landed. Thank God!' It is like something to hang on to where before there was nothing else apart from white sky."[4] Often statements by artists who work within the critical texts of their culture peel off more layers than any interpretative exegesis could ever hope to do. Exactly for this reason McQueen's words require further explication, if only to set them in relation to his critical awareness and productive reading of certain forms of literature in which the figurative, black, Africanist presence looms like such menace. For matters of simple comparison, let us contrast this line: "It is like something to hang on to where before there was nothing else apart from white sky" with these from Poe's ...*Gordon Pym*, "The *darkness* (my emphasis) had materially increased, relieved only by the glare of the water thrown back from the *white* (my emphasis) curtain before us." The imponderable darkness against an elevating whiteness, nothing could be more significant in appraising McQueen's relationship to the paradoxical texts of literary and film representations than this juxtaposition.

6

Even if his work is not just concerned with film as an artistic device, it engages it with such elegant subtlety, that some of his references become lost on even the most attentive audience. It establishes both his intimacy and ambivalence towards narratives of race. Even on a formal level the shot in which the walking figure begins to emerge from the empty white sky into the space filled with trees, reminds one of Rodchenko's *The Pioneer* and *Pine Trees*. The beautiful and resolute way in which the figure emerges into subjecthood, is perhaps another example of McQueen's grasp of the emotional power of cinema. It has always surprised me that very few of McQueen's commentators have been able to pick up on some of these issues and the meaning of his work.

They have been more willing to merely encapsulate the work in autobiographical terms. The acknowledgment of Baldwin, Morrison and Hurston in *Just Above My Head* has very little to do with blackness or autobiography, as many have interpreted this film to be. McQueen rather presents us with the absurdity of the literal evocations of blackness that often accompanies the work of non-caucasian artists. Because his films often have black actors (almost always involving McQueen as the main lead), there is an assumption that they are necessarily about issues of identity. The figurative black presence is thus seen out of context; as an emblematic rather than a nominal

Barrage, 1998

Barrage, 1998

presence. This reading suggests some socio-anthropological angle, a limited concession, it would appear, of narrative intention in the otherwise sparse films. The degree to which McQueen, as a principal agent of his films, serves to further bifurcate the space between a straightforward artistic purpose and a more invidious sense of social documentary, is highlighted in how autobiography as a synechdoche of identity in fact degrades the full understanding of his work.

Nowhere is this taken to a more absurd level than in a review in *The New York Times*, of *Deadpan* (1997), shown in November of that year at the Museum of Modern Art in New York. The reviewer writes about moments in the short film, which drains it of its context and supplements it with his own projection. He writes: "In 'Deadpan', the wall topples again and again, the rate of recurrence accelerating as the film nears its end. Metaphors crowd in. Seen in an American context, the house suggests a sharecropper's cabin; its destruction evokes Abraham Lincoln's Civil War caveat, 'a house divided against itself cannot stand', referring to a nation riven by the question of slavery. (Mr. McQueen is black)." Enough. The critic in question does the most incongruous thing, by shifting radically from the proper reading of the film, to questions of race, which are not even remotely connected to the artist's intention.

I know why the reviewer, a respected critic, would jump to such a quick conclusion. One reason concerns the nature of the black image in popular discourse, especially in film and museum culture. The black image in those contexts, is often read, before anything else, as a political image. Matthew Barney, who stars in all his *Cremaster* films, is perfectly well anchored in the framework of his art, untouched by any facile autobiographical connotations. Cindy Sherman's response to the construction of femininity in her *Untitled Film Stills*, is no more about her as a person than it is about white women. On the other hand, the ways in which the black figure signifies in the broader spectrum of modern and contemporary art, has always had a touch of the anthropological and social documentary imparted to it.

Even if autobiography is not necessarily a handicap, the fact that *Deadpan*, was a response to a moment in film history, a restaged vignette from Buster Keaton's classic genre film *Steamboat Bill Jr.* made the critic's interpretation strange indeed. In the original, an unobserving and oblivious Keaton stands on a spot where a house topples and crashes through him. Shocked into numbness he stands there as if nothing had happened. McQueen found this scene one of the wonderful things that could be done with film; one can take a seemingly silly idea and give it a compelling, powerful emotional resonance. In his version, McQueen had an A-frame house constructed, with one perfect picture window. The film begins with McQueen standing on what appears to be a field with trees dotting the landscape. Slowly the façade of the house topples over and through him. Over and over the same action takes place, but from decidedly different camera perspectives. With each toppled façade no harm comes to the stoic figure, standing in front and in the way of the impending disaster, which manages to leave him unscathed. It is then doubly disturbing that *Deadpan*, which was a critical response to the methods of classic Hollywood genre films is read in such an unambiguous and restrictive manner. As Henry Louis Gates has suggested in his analyses of the black literary tradition, the determining formal relationship between literature and social institutions often encourages a position and attitude which cites and belabours the social and documentary status of black art.[5]

Marking a departure from this overly restrictive tendency to narrow the meaning of the work of so-called black artists, Miles Davis decided at a certain moment to turn his back on his audience while playing his trumpet. Davis's quiet aggression was both a political and artistic act. Like Davis, McQueen is subversive in his usage of political content in his work, because he tricks you into thinking that his films are devoid of specific narrative content. The reality though, is that he subsumes his content in codes which the viewer has to search for. If Davis turned his back on his audience, to let them focus their attention on his music rather than on him (the classic black male stud, 'a walking phallic symbol' as Baldwin memorably put it) performing, McQueen does essentially the same with his silent films, allowing for the raw, emotional, and distilled images of his films to speak on his behalf. With the elliptical and carefully structured films he has made thus far, there is no doubt he has more than succeeded in this endeavour.

NOTES

1. To get some sense of what is being suggested by McQueen's play with realism, see Decarava's *Five Men, Sun and Shade, Dancers* and *Stickball*, or Rodchenko's *To the Demonstration, Ship Timber, On the Pavement, The Telephone*, and *The Fire-escape*.
2. Gilles Deleuze, *Cinema 1, The Movement-Image*, translated by Hugh Tomlison and Barbara Habberjam, Minneapolis, University of Minnesota Press, 1986, p.141.
3. Ibid.
4. "Let's Get Physical: Steve McQueen Interviewed by Patricia Bickers", *Art Monthly*, No. 202, Dec. 1996-Jan. 1997, p.5.
5. Henry Louis Gates Jr., *Figures in Black: Words, Signs, and the 'Racial' Self*, New York and Oxford, Oxford University Press, 1987, p.3.

Bear, 1993
16 mm, black & white film, video transfer. Silent
10 min 35 sec

Five Easy Pieces, 1995
16mm, black & white, colour film, video transfer. Silent
7 min 34 sec

Stage, 1996
35mm, black & white film. Silent
6 min

Just Above My Head, 1996
16mm, black & white film, video transfer. Silent
9 min 35 sec

Exodus, 1992/1997
Super 8 colour film, video transfer. Silent
1 min 5 sec

Catch, 1997
Colour video projection. Silent
1 min 54 sec

Deadpan, 1997
16mm, black & white film, video transfer. Silent
4 min 30 sec

Drumroll, 1998
Colour video projection, triptych. Sound
22 min 1 sec

White Elephant, 1998
107 x 246 cm, 370 kg
Chromed steel roundabout
Installed in pink room
Dimensions variable

Something old, Something new,
Something borrowed, Something blue, 1996 /1998
35mm transfer, 16mm Film Loop
2 min

Barrage, 1998
40 x 50 cm
Series of 59 photographs

STEVE McQUEEN

Born in London, 1969, lives and works in Amsterdam.

1998	DAAD, Berlin
1996	ICA Futures Award
1993-94	Tisch School of the Arts, New York University, New York
1990-93	Goldsmiths' College, London
1989-90	Chelsea School of Art

Solo Exhibitions

1999	ICA, London
	Kunsthalle Zürich
1998	Museum Boijmans Van Beuningen, Rotterdam
	Four Projected Images, Museum of Modern Art, San Francisco
	Galerie Marian Goodman, Paris
1997	Portikus, Frankfurt (cat.)
	Stedelijk Van Abbemuseum, Eindhoven
	Marian Goodman Gallery, New York
	Milwaukee Art Museum, Milwaukee
	Museum of Modern Art, New York
1996	Museum of Contemporary Art, Chicago (cat.)
	Anthony Reynolds Gallery, London

Group Exhibitions (selection)

1999	Museum of Contemporary Art, Houston
1998	*Wounds*, Moderna Museet, Stockholm (cat.)
	Ironisch/Ironic, Museum für Gegenwartskunst, Zürich (cat.)
1997	*Documenta 10*, Kassel (cat.)
	2nd Johannesburg Biennale, Johannesburg (cat.)
	Infra-Slim, The Soros Center for Contemporary Art, Kiev
1996	*Life/Live*, Musée d'Art Moderne de la Ville de Paris, Centro Cultural Belem, Lisbon (cat.)
1996	*Spellbound*, Hayward Gallery, London (cat.)
1995	*Mirage: Enigma of Race, Difference and Desire*, ICA, London (cat.)
	The British Art Show, Manchester and touring (cat.)
1994	*Acting Out: The Body in Video, Then and Now*, Royal College of Art, London (cat.)

INSTITUTE OF CONTEMPORARY ARTS

The Mall, London SW1Y 5AH
Tel(44) (0)171 930 0493 Fax (44) (0)171 873 0051
e-mail:info@ ica.org.uk
http://www.ica.org.uk

Registered charity number 236848

Director: PHILIP DODD
Director of Exhibitions: EMMA DEXTER
Exhibitions Organiser for *Steve McQueen*: SUSAN COPPING
Exhibitions Organiser: KATYA GARCÍA-ANTÓN
Gallery Managers: ANGUS HOWIE, DAVID WILKINSON
Exhibitions Interns: ZOE BINGHAM, JUSTIN MCGUIRK AND ARIELLA YEDGAR

The ICA is financially assisted by The Arts Council of England,
Westminster City Council, British Film Institute and Europa Cinemas

The exhibition is presented with the financial support of the London Arts Board, the
Mondriaan Foundation Amsterdam, for the advancement of the visual arts, design and
museums, The Henry Moore Foundation and the ICA's 50th Anniversary Auction Fund

KUNSTHALLE ZÜRICH

Limmatstr. 270
CH-8005 Zürich
Tel 41 1 272 15 15
Fax 41 1 272 18 88
e-mail: kunsthallezh@access.ch

Curator: BERNHARD BÜRGI
Assistants: BETTINA MARBACH, ANDREA RUMMEL
Technicians: DANIEL HUNZIKER, MARTIN SCHNIDRIG

The Kunsthalle Zürich would like to thank
Schweizerische Rückversicherungs-Gesellschaft

and The British Council